# COACHING OVER COFFEE

Page intentionally left blank

# COACHING OVER COFFEE

*Advice I would give you if we met for a cup of coffee*
*Maria Webb*

Copyright © 2020 Maria Webb
All rights reserved.
ISBN -

# DEDICATION

To Alexia, for always giving me a reason to keep going.

Love, "Mommy Dearest"

# TABLE OF CONTENTS

Dedication
Table of Contents
Introduction
Acknowledgements
Words
Gratitude
Trash To Treasure
Balance
Prioritize
Focus
Self-Care
Getting Things Done
Leverage
Will Power
Success Leaves Clues
Think Big
Collaborate
Financial Review
Alibis
Selfish Is Good
Let It Go

Stop Giving
Transform
Change Is An Inside Job
Are You Ready For Change
Happiness Is A Choice
Are You Willing To Keep Choosing?
Keep Going
References

# INTRODUCTION

My name is Maria Webb. I am an entrepreneur, investor, volunteer, wife, and mother of three children: Alexia, James and Amelia; a mother-in-law to LaMarr, a grandmother to two very spicy grandchildren: LaNiyah and LaMarr. I live in Lexington, Michigan, with my husband, Jim and the two younger children.

I graduated with a BBA and an MBA from Walsh College, one of the most reputable business colleges in Michigan. Being focused on the goal of getting a degree saved me from giving up on myself and my future when I was homeless and living out of my car. Being versatile has led me to careers in logistics, medical administration, teaching, and real estate. Being tenacious has made me successful in life, and being adventurous has led me to travelling the United States, Canada, Mexico, Germany, Spain, and Pakistan.

After many requests for "a minute to meet and get a quick coaching over coffee," I decided to put together the advice I give most often. I hope you enjoy these quick tips. So, grab your coffee or tea and enjoy!

# ACKNOWLEDGEMENTS

Thank you from the top of my head to the tips of my toes to my husband, Jim for never giving up on me. Thank you to my children for the love and hugs that keep me going, even on the toughest days. Thank you to Tracey Pagana for telling me to go for it and write a book. Thank you to Tanya Griffin for the amazing cover art and Susan Talbot for editing. Thank you to my mom, Arlene for always believing in me. Thank you to my Grandma Nelson who showed me how to make things "show up" in my life. Thank you to my grandmother Vanderpool, who always encouraged me to be "better."

Thank you to all the members of the Healing Circle for your kindness and support. Thank you to all my past, current, and future clients for your trust and your referrals. Thank you to my friends and family for your support. All of you have helped me to make a wonderful life full of activity, change, and progress.

# WORDS

The words we use are important. That is why large companies use specific scripts and dialogs for their call centers: to create predictable results for sales and service. The words you speak and the words in your head create results, too. If you spend all your time thinking and talking about how stressful and bad business is, business will be bad and stressful.

If you are in a preschool class for more than five minutes, you will hear the phase, "Use your words." This is important advice for all ages. For preschoolers, it can mean saying "I want a drink" instead of pointing, yelling, or hitting. Teaching the use of words is powerful for all age groups. As adults, using the right words and actions leads to success.

There are many training programs, such as the language of sales, that teach not only the words to use, but also the tone, speed, and emphasis to place on each word. While this training is not for everyone, choosing your words wisely is. Even if you are not in a sales position, the words you use create success or failure for you every day. If you talk about stress, all you see and hear is stress.

We grow into the conversations we have every day, so choose words of hope, encouragement, and opportunity with the VIPs in your life, and you will see change. Start talking about your lives and your businesses with words of opportunity, and answer the door when opportunity comes knocking.

# GRATITUDE

I have two magic words and an easy two-step process to improve your business and your life. The words are so easy to pronounce that, by Kindergarten, every child knows them. The words are: Thank you.

Saying "thank you" is the easy step. The next step is a little harder: actually being thankful. I am not talking about lip service or scripts. I am talking about sincere gratitude. No one is solely a self-made success. Rather, everyone has a mentor, coach, or leader who has helped them along the way. Even Albert Einstein had a mentor who gave him key texts to study and met him for dinner weekly to mentor him. Sam Walton had his father-in-law to lend him money to start his first franchise. For me, it is my family and my team, who have always been supportive and offer positive feedback.

With this in mind, take a minute to write down 10 things or people you are thankful for; then say "thank you" to the people who have made your success possible. Do this today, and you will have a better day. Do it every day, and you will have a better life. Here is a blank form below get you started!

# MY DAILY GRATITUDE LIST

1. _____
2. _____
3. _____
4. _____
5. _____
6. _____
7. _____
8. _____
9. _____
10. _____

*Be quiet for five minutes and ask
for guideance for the day.*

*Send love to those who bother you.*

Proctor Gallagher
INSTITUTE

# TRASH TO TREASURE

My eight-year-old son is always looking for treasure when we go out for walks. This got me thinking of the old saying, "One man's trash is another man's treasure." (Stanley, 2000), 1,300 millionaires were surveyed on the factors that contributed to their success. There was an overriding theme: they each started their businesses by finding a need, filling it, and creatively keeping costs low. One of my favorite examples was turning the trash fabric scraps on the cutting room floor to the treasure of a profitable product: gun cleaning patches. I learned of another excellent example when I attended an economic conference discussing a new type of fuel plant in Sarnia that is producing biofuel from corn stalks and cobs; not the kernel, that is edible, but the stalks and cobs that have always been left behind as trash.

Finding opportunities like these takes looking at life and situations differently and asking yourself, "What here holds value?" Whether it is corn stalks, cow manure, paper, or plastic bottles, I challenge you to look at the world around you with the eyes of value and opportunity, and when opportunity knocks, answer the call.

I had an interesting opportunity come up recently. It was completely unexpected and not quite what I am used to doing. In the past, I would have seen it as interesting, but not for me. This time I asked myself, "How is this for me?"

What opportunities are knocking for you? What doors open if, instead of saying, "That is not for me," you ask yourself "How this is for me?" Remember: to get a new result, you have to choose a

MARIA J WEBB

new response.

# BALANCE

If you are struggling with work/life balance, you are not alone. Over 7,000 newspaper and magazine articles mentioned the topic in the years 2007 to 2011.

In *Suzanne's Diary for Nicholas,* (Patterson, 2001), the personal and professional balancing act is highlighted in this analogy: Imagine life is a game in which you are juggling 5 balls. The balls are called work, family, health, friends, and integrity. You're keeping them all in the air. But, one day, you finally come to understand that work is a rubber ball. If you drop it, it will bounce back. The other 4 balls - family, health, friends, integrity – are made of glass. If you drop one of these, it will be irrevocably scuffed, nicked, perhaps even shattered.

Demands on your time are everywhere. Work too long and your personal life suffers. Too many to do's in your personal life and you feel like you never get a chance to breathe. Focus on the priorities that matter most to you and accept the fact some things will have to be left undone.

# PRIORITIZE

We are all busy, but what are we busy doing? Answering an endless stream of emails? Checking items off a to-do list that is never done?

Don't get trapped in the check off game. Most to-do lists are just basic survival lists and do not lead to success. Rather, they lead you on to tasks that may never produce results. To turn a to-do list into a success list, decide what matters most and focus on it.

Pareto's Principle, or the 80/20 rule states that 80 percent of results come from 20 percent of effort. From (Keller, 2013)a business book that is based on the 80/20 rule, I have borrowed these two big ideas: 1. Go small, but find what matters most and focus on it. 2. Take the 80/20 rule to the extreme. Keep asking yourself what gets the most results until you have the one thing you should focus on. Sometimes, it will be the first thing you do; sometimes, it is the only thing you do.

# FOCUS

So many of us are in a productivity-killing trap. We have bought into the myth that we must multitask, believing it is the only way to get things done in this hectic, fast-paced world. So, we go through our days with our phones never out of reach. While we work, eat, or play, we are checking e-mails, text messages, social media, or games. It is a miracle there aren't more accidents, with the constant distractions. We, all, are going big, trying to do everything, looking for the next app or technology to get more done, when what we really need is to go small to achieve big success. In the best-selling book *The One Thing*, research of over 1,000 scholarly articles and journals showed that the most successful people focused on one thing with purpose and became successful. Think of Steve Jobs, Bill Gates, or Michael Phelps.

With that in mind, what is the one thing you can do in your business that will result in everything else becoming easier or unnecessary?

# SELF-CARE

In the book, (Covey, 2013), the seventh habit is "sharpening the saw." The basic concept is you cannot cut wood with a dull saw. As a result, work must stop to sharpen the saw. It is easy enough to grasp the concept of keeping tools in good condition to achieve the best results. Applying this habit in your life requires attention to all four parts of you:

1. The physical body, including exercise and stress management
2. The social and emotional components, including service and socializing
3. The spiritual being, including clarifying your values and experiencing quiet time
4. The mental faculties, including reading and planning.

Take time to take care of all four parts of you, or time will take care of you. If you put off the rest, exercise, and stress management now, you pay in the long run with health issues. Take the stairs, drink more water, have lunch with a friend, read engaging and uplifting books. When you come to the end of your life, do you want to say, "I'm so glad I did," or "I'm so sorry I didn't?"

# GETTING THINGS DONE

So much to do, so little time. The day is full of tasks, chores, projects. You rush through the day, putting out fires and furiously answering texts, e-mails, and phone calls. You get home exhausted and not quite sure where the day went, with a to-do list that seems like it has grown. There are only 24 hours in a day, but even if there were 30 hours, without a plan and a system the extra hours would not make a difference.

*Getting Things Done*, (Allen, 2015), is a great tool, with step-by-step instructions to build a simple system to get your work done in a relaxed way. There are two goals in the system:

1. Collect all your tasks into an external organizational system, and
2. Self-discipline to put new tasks in the system as they arise.

The goal is to have all the tasks in a system and out of your head, so you can gain focus and clarity. So, how do you get in the zone to conquer your tasks effectively and sanely? Let's start with tying up loose ends of unfinished items. The items can be as big as growing your business or picking up bread.

There are three actions to take with every item:

1. Get the item into your choice of system: paper, app, or smartphone
2. Review the item and note the due date
3. Review your system regularly according to your needs, i.e.

morning, twice per day, or hourly

To create a system that allows you to go through these three steps quickly, chose a system that you will use. Decide on a paper system or an app, like Evernote. A simple file system of 12 folders (months), each with 28 to 31 folders (days of the month) works very well. Items are sorted by month and day. This system works on paper or electronically. Once tasks are collected, file them according to due date.

It's time to collect the tasks so they are in a system and off your mind. E-mails are collected electronically in an In Box or a note-taking app; others, you must collect in paper form. Once you choose your method, collect everything from work projects to grocery lists. Stick to your method, and keep it simple.

For an effective to-do list, use one sheet of paper for each task on your list for easy sorting and prioritizing. This could take some time, and you may need to lock yourself in with no distractions to get this step done. Once the items are collected, process them by asking:

1. Can I take action on this?

If no, you can: (i) Throw it out, (ii) reference it (think menus), or (iii) file it for review.

If yes, ask yourself: (i) Can it be completed in two minutes or less?

If yes, do it now.

If no, determine the next step.

If you can delegate it, do it immediately.

If you must complete it yourself, write the next step in the calendar on the appropriate follow-up date and file in your system.

# LEVERAGE

How do you get the work on your to-do list done, let alone make it to a couple of dinners or time out with friends? In a word: leverage. Leverage is not just for finances. It is a powerful tool to create more time and success in business and relationships. So, how do you leverage time?

Group activities that have similar tasks. For example, if you are cooking one meal, prep items for tomorrow's meal at the same time. If you are really ambitious, get the cookbook, ***Once a Month Cooking*** (Lagerborg, 2009). It contains the grocery lists, menus, prep steps and packaging tips to do one day of shopping and prep and one day of cooking for 30 days of meals. For business tasks, look at the items you do every day and delegate those that are simple and require less skill, like running errands, to assistants or interns.

Leverage your connections by asking peers for information on conferences and educational opportunities. Leverage your talent and skills by continually practicing or improving the scope of what you know. This can help you in your career, but how about a way to help at home? Do you enjoy painting and want to practice a new technique, but need an area to try it out? Find a friend who paints and has a skill you do not have. Leverage your education by taking advantage of networking opportunities with alumni or association groups. Alumni groups can have connections to recruiters and business owners if you are looking for employment, and associations have access to resources they are often happy to share. This can be as easy as joining the alumni Facebook group or as involved as joining the alumni group and attending functions.

If you have tried leveraging, but are not sure if it is worth continuing, consider joining a professional or business networking group. If you already know of a network of accountants, lawyers, electricians, and contractors, consider forming a business networking group involving all of the individual groups, not only for leverage, but also for business referrals. If you currently are not a member of a network or if you want to expand your current network, check with your local area Chamber of Commerce for events. This is a great way to meet new business associates, talk about and give referrals, and find out about community events. Give it a try! I, personally, have found these events to be very worthwhile.

Good luck, and I hope these tips give you more time for the VIPs in your life.

# WILL POWER

As the saying goes, "Where there is a will, there is a way." Some view will power as the source of strength and success. What most fail to understand is this: will power is not always on "will call." Will power seems simple: Invoke my will, and I will get my way. The only problem is that without the discipline and habits in place, will power is not predictable or dependable. Will power takes mental energy to invoke.

The ***Journal of Personality and Social Psychology***® (Cooper, 2020) detailed nine studies on nutrition and will power. The studies concluded that will power is a muscle that does not bounce back quickly. The keys to developing will power are timing and rest. Will power is like the battery on your phone: every time you use it, you have less power left. The good news is, will power is rechargeable. Proper rest, diet, and exercise are the energy that powers your will back up. So, whatever the most important task of the day is, do it first while you have the most will power and focus.

# SUCCESS LEAVES CLUES

There are many sayings that sound like the truth, but are not factual. For example, put a frog in lukewarm water, and you can slowly raise the temperature without the frog's noticing. Not true! How many times have we heard that successful people are disciplined and lead a disciplined life? The truth is, success is achieved by using discipline just long enough for habit to kick in. Success is about training yourself on the right actions until the actions become routine and the routine becomes habit. So, how do we create the right habits? Find the routines that successful people follow, put them into your schedule, and practice them for 66 days until the routines become your habit.

Success leaves clues, and there is much documentation on the subject. **The 7 Habits of Highly Successful People** is one good source. The website, www.the1thing.com has a list of research, books, and articles on the subject. Reading and research are everywhere, but the key is to decide on your goals, pick a plan, and start!

There are thousands of books, articles and blogs dedicated to goal setting. Some suggest paper; some suggest apps for your phone. The best system is the one you will use. One size does not fit all, so use the format that works for you. The key is to set a goal and an end date; then break the goal down into stages or steps, to be accomplished in one week, one month, and so on. Then, start working on these smaller steps. Small changes lead to big results.

# THINK BIG

Would you be willing to send your child to a coach or tutor who told them to think small because they would never achieve above a certain level? Why would you give yourself the same advice? No one knows their limit for achievement, so why waste time thinking small? There are many stories of businesses and inventors with little to no money that have attained great success. When JK Rowling started writing Harry Potter, she envisioned seven years of books.

In order to achieve big success, you have to think big and act according to your big plans. No one has more time in the day than anyone else, and working harder does not equal more results. Sometimes, what seems impossible when you start is easier to accomplish than you anticipate. Big stands for greatness and living your best life. This means different goals to each one of us, but the end result is a life worth living.

Think big. What does this mean? How do you know if you are thinking big? Here are four tips from the bestselling book, ***The One Thing***:

1. *A rule of thumb is whatever your goal is, double it. If your goal is 10, think how do I reach 20?*
2. *Don't order off the menu. To quote Apple's 1997 Think differently campaign: "Einstein, Hitchcock and Gandhi thought differently and people who are crazy enough to think they can change the world are the only ones who do."*

3. *Act boldly. Thinking without action accomplishes nothing. Imagine what your best life looks like. Can't imagine it? Research the people who are successful. Success leaves clues. What are the habits of success?*
4. *Don't fear failure. Extraordinary results are built on failures as well as results. When you fail, stop and ask what worked and what didn't. Learn from your mistakes and grow.*

Some of the most successful people experienced big failures along the way: Ford, Lincoln, Edison. Failure is part of learning and, ultimately, success.

# COLLABORATE

The economy and competition have changed the way all of us do business in some way or another. The best and most exciting change I see is the pooling of talents and resources to promote the unique and beautiful region in which I live and work as a great place to visit, work, and play. There are many groups with great missions that overlap in some way. The exciting part is seeing the groups working together to achieve their goals by sharing resources, including some of the most valuable resources: budgets and volunteers. It is a work in progress and there are challenges, but the challenges are worth the results. With this in mind, where are your opportunities to collaborate?

# FINANCIAL REVIEW

Every year at tax time, many of us undertake the process of compiling receipts for the accountants. During this time of financial review, it is a good time to take a minute to review your finances and plan for your future. Even if you total your receipts with a calculator, stop and look at your total income and spending and ask if you are saving enough to fund your retirement.

Not sure what you need to save to fund your retirement lifestyle? Do a quick calculation at AARP.org. Then, take action. The best option is always an automatic deduction, preferably a payroll deduction you set up once that is pre-tax. Your employer does not have a retirement plan? Call your local bank. Most have IRA options that allow you to set up an automatic checking account deduction.

Whatever options you choose, make a choice and take action. Keep in mind, most millionaires in the United States are regular people who lived on a budget and took 10 to 20 percent of their income and invested it in real estate, the stock market, and their businesses.

# ALIBIS

Do any of these alibis sound familiar? I would be successful:

> If I didn't have a wife and family...
> If I had enough pull...
> If I had money...
> If I had time...
> If I had been given a chance...
> If I were younger...
> If other people didn't 'have it in for me'...
> If times were better...
> If other people understood me...
> If I were free...
> If I had someone to help me...
> If I could just get out of debt...
> IF ****and this is the greatest of them all***

> I had the courage to see myself as I really am, I would *find out what is wrong with me and correct it,* then I might have a chance to profit by my mistakes and learn something from the experience of others for I know there is something wrong with me, or I would not be where *I would have been* if I had spent more time analyzing my weaknesses and less time building alibis to cover them."

Excerpt from ***Think and Grow Rich*** (Hill, 2012)

# SELFISH IS GOOD

What if being selfish was a good thing?

Is being selfish a bad thing? Who is selfish? The one who takes care of themselves OR the one who EXPECTS you to take care of them? It is a matter of perspective.

It's time to write your story! You choose how you see your life. Is it a life of futile struggle or hard-won success? Choose to write the story of your life the way you want it. Are you writing a horror story or an inspirational movie? You get to choose.

What are you doing to care for YOU to make your goals a reality?

# LET IT GO

When you are surrounded by family, friends and others who are "a mess," who just "need your help," please remember:

You cannot get sick enough to make anyone else well. You cannot get poor enough to make someone else rich. You cannot lead from behind. You have to take care of yourself to be a good leader. Consider this: Why is it selfish to take care of yourself, but NOT selfish for someone else to expect you to take care of them?

My challenge to you is to let it go. Let go of the worry, the control, and the story. Let it go and take care of yourself before you go to save anyone else. If you need more sleep, sleep. If you need to exercise, exercise! You cannot pour from an empty cup!

# STOP GIVING

I have to confess, I used to be a giver. I would give at the office. I would give at home. I would feel guilty if I did not have any change to give to anyone ringing a bell or with a can collecting for a cause. I would give to anyone who said they needed my help. Need help moving furniture and organizing your house? Sure!

I always believed that I had to give to receive; that if I were physically or financially able, I had to help. And I was tired and sometimes resentful of all the giving.

Then one day, I had a conversation that changed my perception. If you give, they will always keep taking and rejecting. If you GIFT, they can receive or reject ONCE. Wow! What a difference two letters make.

Are you willing to gift AND receive?

# TRANSFORM

Messages from the butterfly: Transform!

Butterflies have been following me since my trip to Sacramento, CA, where I started the process of settling my Aunt Ida's estate.

First on stamps; then on stationery, the brochures from the mortuary, the pictures on the walls of Vital Statistics; then on my walks.

What is the message the butterflies want to impress on us? Soar? Transform?

What messages does the butterfly hold for you? Where in your life do you want to soar or transform?

# CHANGE IS AN INSIDE JOB

I let go of my perfect plan and took an opportunity that seemed like it fell into my lap. Keep in mind, my perfect plan involved a lot of work - HARD work! In my head, success equals hard work. The perfect plan was a PLAN! I had action steps, systems, demographics, a routine. I kept my business life strictly business and my personal life personal. I had to change the story in my head to change the results I could see around me.

Through an interesting series of events - a chance meeting on a retreat, a small gift, sharing a cool tool with a friend – all of the sudden, I was invited to a sold-out expo to sell and speak about a tool I was not yet 100 percent ready to publicly promote to my business network because it would mean making my personal beliefs public.

I had to let go of my fear of judgement to receive this opportunity. I had been working very hard to grow and network and attract that perfect client in my perfect plan. I attended over 40 events in 30 days, three of which I facilitated. I was exhausted!

When I said yes to this new opportunity, the booth was added, and I was able to get advertising and a speaking spot. When I said yes, the production and shipping process was put into place. When I said yes, the payment processing system, assistance with the booth, time to go, and a two-bedroom suite for the event showed up! When I said yes, my personal time and business time were fun and creative together. When I said yes, my family joined in instead of feeling left out.

What are you afraid of that, if you faced it, would transform your life?

# ARE YOU READY FOR CHANGE

Not sure what to do next, but you are ready, willing, and seeking whatever you have to do to get better results? Notice I did not include "able" because you are always able. I had been ready, willing, and seeking something different professionally for years, but never found anything but hard work and burn-out.

The tipping point for me was when I started feeling sick and tired, every day. That is when I went from settling for "good enough" to asking, "What is it going to take for me to have the life I want?" I started looking for a holistic approach to my health and found a chiropractor who suggested I look for a less stressful business, as I walked in, a ball of tension, for adjustments. Life is unpredictable. Once I started asking, "What is it going to take," it led to more questions and letting go of having the perfect plan.

This led me to a questioning what was the common theme of everything I had done professionally? What did working in a variety of fields, including import manager, medical office manager, college instructor, real estate sales, and investment have in common? All of these fields of endeavor have a common theme of continuously setting and reaching goals for myself and helping others to do the same. That is when I decided to make the career shift from real estate to coaching. I started collaborating with others in my network who were motivational speakers and coaches, set up a limited liability company, and facilitated my first international experience retreat 90 days later: ReModel Your

Habits, ReModel Your Life (ReModel International, 2018).

I had a specific client in mind: female, 35-55, professional, looking to grow a new or existing business. These are the clients who showed up for the retreat; these were the clients in my comfort zone. This retreat is where I was gifted my first heart-shaped, pocket-size orgonite from a shaman, Gregor (Kocijancic, 2020). It was the last days of the retreat, and I was leaving for home the next day. When I held the orgonite, I could feel the electrical energy. I asked what it was; however, he was not there to explain. The others said it was for putting by cell phones or WiFi routers to keep the radiation waves from bothering you while you sleep. I thought there had to be more to it, so I started seeking more information. This seeking lead to more change.

Gregor sent me information on the plates he makes to clean food and water. I wanted to test it, so I ordered a plate specifically to use for food, water, and meditation. At this point, I still was not 100 percent sure what this tool was, but I wanted it. I ordered four more of the small hearts and one large plate. I started using the plate with avocados and tomatoes and noticed they were staying fresher longer. Then, I started experimenting with putting a glass of water on the plate, and the water tasted better. My daughter placed the plate under her bed and had the best sleep she had had in years. I used this new tool for over three months before I shared it with my energy healing groups. (Gregor Kocijanic, 2020)

Once I started seeing more and more results, I decided to get over my fear of judgement and share the plates with a healing group. Although these ladies were in my target market for coaching and I was willing to sell coaching services to them, I unintentionally sold five custom orgonite orders that night. I had no intention or any contract to sell; Gregor was not even my target coaching client. I only felt an openness to share what I had learned about this amazing product. All I knew was this was a product people were ready, willing, and seeking to buy. This was the classic "see a need and fill it," so I began coaching Gregor on the online ordering and import/export processes, as all of his orders to that point had been single orders that were hand delivered. This client, whom I was not seeking intentionally, came into my path because I was ready and able, with a unique background: import/export, health and wellness, sales, and teaching.

What is seeking you in your path that you are ready and able to seize? And are you willing to let go of your perfect plan to seize it?

# HAPPINESS IS A CHOICE

What if happiness is a choice?

What choice for happiness do you have available that, if you made it, would create a greater life, a greater reality for you, and a greater world for us all?

That is a question I am asking and would love to share some easy ways to make happiness your daily reality!

I understand that if you are in a place in your life where happiness seems impossible, this may all sound crazy. But what if something else were possible? What if the idea that your problems keep you from being happy is one of the biggest lies we buy?

What is it you can choose today that will bring you happiness right away?

Ask and choose it – even if it is just for 10 minutes!

Check out the link below for 4 tools to use right now.

https://www.accessconsciousness.com/en/get-your-happy-on/ (Heer, 2020)

# ARE YOU WILLING TO KEEP CHOOSING?

One day, I made a choice to get a business degree. Based on that choice, I decided I had to be professional, serious, practical, and live by the book. In other words, I had to fit in the "business box." So, I took all the classes, got good grades, graduated from a good business college, and went to work for a huge international company with lots of promotion potential. Everything that I was taught to do in school, I did. I kept making career choices based on the path to success I was taught in school. I was getting the same results I had experienced in other endeavors: fatigue and frustration. So, I kept making choices until I eventually chose to start my own business.

I am going to let you in on a secret: once you make a choice, you can keep choosing. You don't just choose one time and then never choose again. Every day, when you get up, you choose to make your bed, or not. You choose to eat healthy, or not. You choose to exercise, or not. You choose to go to that same job, or not. No one forces you. You choose to have the life you want and to do the work you need to keep that life, or not. Insanity is making the same choices and expecting different results.

So, back to my "business story." I kept making choices that were based on fitting into the "professional business box" I had created with the first choice of my degree. As a result, I was not experiencing much change. I did not take opportunities because I judged them to be not professional enough or not mainstream enough. Then, I received a message from a past client, who has become a friend, telling me to call ASAP - it was urgent! I called her right away. She asked me, "Are you sitting down? Because you better sit down before you fall down!" She had arranged an invitation for me to attend as a vendor, selling orgonite at a Healing Body and Spirit (Stephen, 2019), where the vendor tables were already sold out. At first, I thought, "That's nice, but I don't make the orgonite. I use it and I have helped create the ordering and delivery process for it, but I do not belong as a vendor at a Mind and Body Expo. Business expos, trade shows for realtors, those I have done. Those fit in the "business box."

On the phone with Tracey that day, I made a different choice. I chose to step out of my "business box story." I had been hiding all the other abilities that were not "main stream business-related." Instead of just attending the show and selling a product as a favor for a friend and feeling weird because of the venue, I decided to see it as an opportunity: an opportunity to showcase the product as a tool I use in my business, how I use it, and how I assisted the friend, who is now a client, in expanding his passion into his business.

My question to you is: What are you making wrong about you that, if it were right, would transform your world? And everything that is keeping you from making it right, will you let that go?

# KEEP GOING

Your dream has to be bigger than the excuse. When you wake up weary, you have to know why: Why am I doing so much? Why am I trying so hard?

When I want to give up, often my Grandmother Vanderpool comes into my mind. She experienced many failures and obstacles to get close to her dream of providing both physical and spiritual food for the lost and hurting. She created a legacy for her children.

My grandparents had 15 children between them when they homesteaded a 104-acre dairy farm. My father still owns 10 acres of the original farm.

If anyone was tired, she was tired. If anyone was worn out from caring for others, she was worn out. So, when I wake up weary, I just have to think of Grandma Vanderpool and then get back up and continue on my mission, and so can you! Just because you take a break, doesn't mean you are done. Keep going! The world needs you and your gifts!

# REFERENCES

Allen, D. (2015). *Getting Things Done: The Art of Stress-Free Productivity.* New York, London: Penguin Books.

Cooper, S. K. (2020, April 4). *American Psychological Association.* Retrieved from https://www.apa.org/pubs/journals/psp/: https://www.apa.org/pubs/journals/psp/

Covey, S. (2013). *The 7 Habits of Highly Effective People.* New York City: Simon & Schuster.

Gregor Kocijanic. (2020, May 18). *http://www.gregor.love/personalize-your-orgonite/.* Retrieved from http://www.gregor.love/: http://www.gregor.love/personalize-your-orgonite/

Heer, D. D. (2020, April 4). *Access Consciousness.* Retrieved from Access Consciousness: https://www.accessconsciousness.com/en/get-your-happy-on/

Hill, N. (2012). *Think and Grow Rich.* New York City: Fall River Press.

Keller, G. (2013). *The One Thing.* Austin: Bard Press.

Kocijancic, G. (2020, April 4). *The Wayshower.* Retrieved from The Wayshower: www.gregor.love

Lagerborg, M. B. (2009). *Once-A-Month Cooking Family Favorites.* New York City: St. Martin's Griffin.

Patterson, J. (2001). *Suzanne's Diary for Nicholas.* New York City: Little, Brown & Co.

ReModel International. (2018, 03 10). *www.fuertebalance/retreats.com.* Retrieved from https://remodelinternational.com/.

Stanley, D. T. (2000). *The Millionaire Mind.* Kansas City: Andrews McMeel Publishing.

Stephen, B. (2019, March 01). *Healing Body and Spirit.* Retrieved from Healing Body and Spirit: http://www.healingbody-andspirit.com/

www.ingramcontent.com/pod-product-compliance
Lightning Source LLC
Chambersburg PA
CBHW031506040426
42444CB00007B/1232